UNDERSTANDING DIVINE JUDGMENT

*God has already begun judging his own people.
And if his judgment begins with us, imagine how terrible
it will be for those who refuse to obey his message.*

1 Peter 4:17 *CEV*

by
Franklin N. Abazie

Understanding Divine Judgment
COPYRIGHT 2016 BY Franklin N Abazie
ISBN: 978-1-94513316-9

All right reserved. This book or any portion thereof may not be reproduced or used in any manner whatsoever without the express written permission of the publisher, except for the use of brief quotations in a book review. All Bible quotes are from King James Version and others as noted.

Published by: F N ABAZIE PUBLISHING HOUSE—
aka, Empowerment Bookstore

That I may publish with the voice of thanksgiving and tell of all thy wondrous works.
Psalm 26:7

To order additional copies, wholesales or booking call:
the Church office (973-372-7518)
or Empowerment Bookstore Hotline (973-393-8518)

Worship address:
343 Sanford Avenue, Newark, New Jersey 07106
Administrative Head Office address:
33 Schley Street Newark New Jersey 07112
Email: pastorfranknto@yahoo.com
Website www.fnabaziehealingministries.org
Publishing House: www.fnabaziepublishinghouse.org

This book is a production of F N Abazie Publishing House. A publication Arms of Miracle of God Ministries 2016.
First Edition

CONTENTS

THE MANDATE OF THE COMMISSION....................iv
ARMS OF THE COMMISSION...................................v
INTRODUCTION...vi
CHAPTER 1
God's Divine Warning..1
CHAPTER 2
The Purpose of Redemption...................................14
CHAPTER 3
Salvation—The Escape Route to Eternal Life..........30
CHAPTER 4
Prayer of Salvation..52
ABOUT THE AUTHOR..58

THE MANDATE OF THE COMMISSION

"The moment is due to impact your world through the revival of the healing & miracle ministry of Jesus Christ of Nazareth.

"I am sending you to restore health unto thee and I will heal thee of thy wounds, said the Lord of Host."

ARMS OF THE COMMISSION

1) F N Abazie Ministries—Miracle of God Ministries (Miracle Chapel Intl)

2) F N Abazie TV Ministries: Global Television Ministry Outreach

3) F N Abazie Radio Ministries: Radio Broadcasting Outreach

4) F N Abazie Publishing House: Book Publication

5) F N Abazie Bible School: also called Word of Healing Bible School (W.O.H.B.S.)

6) F N Abazie Evangelistic Ass: Miracle of God Ministries: Global Crusade

7) Empowerment Bookstore: Book distribution

8) F N Abazie Helping Hands: Meeting the Help of the Needy Worldwide

9) F N Abazie Disaster Recovery Mission: Global Disaster Recovery

10) F N Abazie Prison Ministry: Prison Ministry For All Convicts "Second Chance"

Some of our ministry arms are awaiting the appointed time to commence.

INTRODUCTION

Although most of us live in denial, none of us will escape **the judgment throne** of the Almighty God. Irrespective of our position in life or influence in the society, we shall all face the judgment throne of God. Every one of us will appear before the judgment throne of God, and we shall all be judged accordingly. In these dreadful days we live in, we must all REPENT of our SINS and begin to live a RIGHTEOUS life. Most of us lack the understanding of **divine judgment**, believe it from the scriptures, we shall all face the judgment throne of God someday.

The America college heritage dictionary defines judgment as follows: The act or process of judging. The formation of an opinion after consideration or deliberation. The mental ability to perceive and distinguish relationships, discernment. The capacity to form an opinion by distinguishing and evaluating. The capacity to assess situation or circumstances and draw sound conclusion. Good sense. An opinion or estimate formed after consideration or deliberation. A formal or authoritative decision. Law: A determination of a court of law, judicial decision.

An assertion of something believed: A misfortune believe to be sent by God as punishment for sin.

The Amplified bible says—

For we [believers will be called to account and]

must all appear before the judgment seat of Christ, so that each one may be repaid for what has been done in the body, whether good or bad that is, each will be held responsible for his actions, purposes, goals, motives—the use or misuse of his time, opportunities and abilities.
2 Corinthians 5:10

Most of us, live life, like there is no punishment for our evil actions. It has been revealed by THE SPIRIT OF GOD in this book that God will judge us all for all our action (good, and evil).

Regardless of how sin, or any evil was committed, God will certainly judge us all. *And thy Father, which seeth in secret, shall reward thee openly.* (Matthew 6:18)

*Great in counsel, and mighty in work:
for thine eyes are open upon all the ways
of the sons of men: to give every one according
to his ways, and according to the fruit of his doings.*
Jeremiah 32:19

God's eye is open upon all our ways. No matter how much we tend to pretend or cover up our evil intention. Beware! GOD will judge all our evil thoughts.

Jesus said in Mark 7:18-23—*And he saith unto them, Are ye so without understanding also? Do ye not perceive, that whatsoever thing from without entereth into the man, it cannot defile him; Because it entereth not into his heart, but into the belly, and goeth out into the draught, purg-*

ing all meats? And he said, That which cometh out of the man, that defileth the man. For from within, out of the heart of men, proceed evil thoughts, adulteries, fornications, murders, Thefts, covetousness, wickedness, deceit, lasciviousness, an evil eye, blasphemy, pride, foolishness: All these evil things come from within, and defile the man.

Knowing that whatsoever good thing any man doeth, the same shall he receive of the Lord, whether he be bond or free.
Ephesians 6:8

The above scripture is a word to you if you are truly sincere to yourself. It takes a change of heart to do the right thing at the right time. It takes contentment to deny all that this dialectic materialistic world has to offer. It takes integrity to walk in the fullness of Gods plan and purpose over your life. We are not only saying for you to hear and repent but for you to have a change of heart that will affect someone else next to you.

For what shall it profit a man, if he shall gain the whole world, and lose his own soul? Or what shall a man give in exchange for his soul?
Mark 8:37-38

Hell is real. Heaven is certain. We all must make the right plan in this present life to make it into heaven (eternity).

*But let every man prove his own work,
and then shall he have rejoicing in himself alone,
and not in another. For every man
shall bear his own burden*
Galatians 6:4-5

Learn to do well.
Isaiah 1:17

Happy reading!

CHAPTER 1
GOD'S DIVINE WARNING

By faith Noah, being warned of God of things not seen as yet, moved with fear, prepared an ark to the saving of his house.
Hebrews 11:7

GOD is WARNING every one of us alive on Earth today of HIS impending **divine judgment** to come—although the excitement of living life has made almost every one of us forget about the **judgment throne of God**. As long as we live, eventually we shall all stand trial before the **judgment throne of God** someday.

Despite living in this dispensation of **grace**, God's divine judgment is inevitable for all men.

And as it is appointed unto men once to die, but after this the judgment.
Hebrews 9:27

Although most of us believers live like we will never die and appear before the **righteous judge**, God's judgment is inevitable as long as we exist. Scriptures tell us that none of us shall escape it. Both the rich and the poor, the tall and the short, regardless of your race tribe and religion—GOD WILL JUDGE US ALL AT

THE END OF OUR LIVES.

The god of this world (Satan) deceives most of us with invisible traps which cannot be seen with the naked eye. But **God's divine judgment** is for our deliverance and exoneration from the accusation of the enemy. It will grant us eternity with JESUS CHRIST in **heaven**. David pleaded for vindication when he cried unto God in Psalms 35:24—*Judge me; O Lord my God according to thy righteousness; and let them not rejoice over me.*

> *Judge me, O God and plead my cause against an ungodly nation. O deliver me from the deceitful and unjust man.*
> **Psalms 43:1**

As believers, we are responsible and accountable for all our actions (thoughts, works, deed, etc.). Whether we did good or evil in our lifetime, we must all be held responsible and accountable for all our actions. No man can escape from the presence of the all wise GOD, who is the **judge** of the **Earth**. **God's divine judgment** is the settlement for how we lived our lives.

Righteousness is the answer against the judgment of God. Until you begin to practice righteousness, you will remain prey and a victim to the accuser of the brethren (Satan). Righteousness delivers and vindicates. God is a righteous judge who will judge every human being at the end of his or her life. Abraham asked a sincere question in Genesis 18:25—*Shall not the judge of all the Earth do right?* God is warning all believers to take heed, lest you will be judged.

*Great in counsel and mighty in work; for thine eyes
are open upon all the ways of the sons of men;
to give every one according to the fruit of his doings.*
Jeremiah 32:19

We live in an end time generation that has IGNORED and NEGLECTED the warning signs of **the judgment throne of GOD**. Familiar scriptures like Galatian 6:5—*For every man shall bear his own burden*—has been greatly IGNORED and NEGLECTED. Believe me, we all shall face the judgment of God and give accounts of our actions and how we lived our lives here on Earth.

*He that hath an ear, let him hear what the Spirit
saith unto the churches; He that overcometh
shall not be hurt of the second death.*
Revelation 2:11

GOD's divine judgment is the second death, according to the above scripture. To make it into heaven with Jesus Christ, we must all strive to avert **God's divine judgment** and be exempted from damnation and hell fire. Remember, second death means "HELL FIRE."

Contrary to what we've heard from the atheist and other scholars that don't know God, **the judgment of God** is certain, it is inevitable, and we must all appear before HIM individually. The Lord shall judge the people. *Judge me, O Lord, according to my righteousness, and according to mine integrity that is in me.* (Psalms 7:8) *And he shall judge the world in righteousness, he shall minister judgment to the people in uprightness.* (Psalms 9:8)

> *Even as I have seen, they that plow iniquity and sow wickedness, reap the same.*
> **Job 4:8**

> *He that soweth iniquity shall reap vanity.*
> **Provers 22:8**

> *Ye have plowed wickedness, ye have reaped iniquity.*
> **Hosea 10:13**

Irrespective of our accomplishments in life—**money**, **fame**, **power**—whether we do evil or good, we WILL be judged. None of us will be spared for our actions based on any merit or abundance of money. There is no bribery, no kick-backs, concerning God's judgment. If we are to make heaven, we must live right.

If we must merit to be exempted, we must **live righteously**, we must **obey the holy Bible** and **apply scriptural commandments** to our every day life.

> *A divine sentence is in the lip of the king; his mouth transgressed not in judgment.*
> **Proverbs 16:10**

REMEMBER—

The Almighty God is the King of Kings and the Lord of Lords. The Bible attested that where the word of the king is, there is **power**.

Every time God speaks, **he backs His word with power**. Have you not heard? *Who is he that saith and it cometh to pass, when the Lord commanded it not?* (Lamentations 3:37)

WHAT ARE WE SAYING?

What we are saying here is for you to REPENT OF YOUR SINS, you must change how you approach material things—especially when dealing with other people. It is time to change how we live our lives. All our evil thoughts GOD WILL JUDGE. It is high time we change our heart. It takes a change of heart to have a transformed life.

Then shall ye return, and discern between the righteous and the wicked, between him that serveth God and him that serveth him not.
Malachi 3:18

Then comes God's judgment—

*For behold the day cometh that shall
burn as an oven; and all the proud,
yea and all that do wickedly shall be stubble;
and the day that cometh shall burn them up
saith the Lord of Host, that it shall leave them
neither root nor branch.*
Malachi 4:1-2

GOD'S JUDGMENT IS INEVITABLE

*For the time is come that judgment must begin at the
house of God: and if it first begin at us, what shall the
end be of them that obey not the gospel of God?*
1 Peter 4:17

Most of us live and pretend as if we will never be judged of our actions. With GOD'S JUDGMENT there is no exemption. GOD WILL JUDGE ALL OF US. (From the PASTOR to the CONGREGATION). *The time is come that judgment must begin at the house of God. And if it first begin at us, what shall the end be of them that obey not the gospel of God?* (1 Peter 4:17)

*Sow to yourselves in righteousness, reap in mercy;
break up your fallow ground: for it is time to seek the
Lord, till he come and rain righteousness upon you.*

Hosea 10:12

> *But seek ye first the kingdom of God, and his righteousness; and all these things shall be added unto you.*
> **Matthew 6:33**

God loves us and wants us to seek His kingdom forever more. God, out of his love for the world (mankind), desires for us all to make it into **heaven** at last so that we will enjoy **eternity with him**.

> *He that doeth righteousness is righteous, even as he is righteous.*
> **1 John 3:7**

Righteousness is not some invented theory, it is not some New Age doctrine. Righteousness is the scriptural demands of the word of God to avert all divine judgment.

In these end times, so many people do not believe in God. I do not agree with Napoleon Bonaparte's quote on religion— *"Religion is excellent stuff for keeping common people quiet."* Oftentimes, most people that do not know of God make whatever comment that they delight in. The Bible says, *"the Lord has made all things for himself; yea even the wicked for the day of evil."* (Proverbs 16:4) Napoléon also said— *"Religion is what keeps the poor from murdering the rich."*

God is Spirit and we shall all be judged in the spiritual court of God (judgment throne of God).

How does God warn us?

Son of man, I have made thee a watchman unto the house of Israel: therefore hear the word at my mouth, and give them warning from me.
Ezekial 3:17

There are several channels through which the most high God warns us—including through DREAMS and VISION, through REVELATION and through the PROPHET.

HOW GOD WARNS US

1) THROUGH THE PROPHET: God uses all his prophets (including pastors, apostles, teachers and evangelists). GOD is sovereign , therefore JEHOVAH will use whosoever that pleases him to call us to **issue divine warning**. *Son of man, I have made thee a watchman unto the house of Israel: therefore hear the word at my mouth, and give them warning from me.* (Ezekiel 3:17)

2) THROUGH DREAMS & VISIONS: One of the greatest access points for us to hear directly from God's throne is through our own dreams and visions. *For God speaketh once, yea twice, yet man perceiveth it not. In a dream, in a vision of the night, when deep sleep falleth upon men, in slumberings upon the bed.* (Job 33:14-15) God uses our dreams and visions to reveal to us a coming blessing and to warn us against impending danger. *After these things the word of the Lord came unto Abram in a vision, saying, Fear not, Abram: I am thy shield, and thy exceeding great reward.* (Genesis 15:1)

3) THROUGH REVELATION: Every time we are in the **spirit**, we **hear** from **God**. For as long as we operate in the **spirit**, we have the advantage to **hear** from **God**. *I was in the Spirit on the Lord's day, and heard behind me a great voice, as of a trumpet.* (Revelation 1:10)

GOD'S WARNINGS IN THE BIBLE

NOAH & HIS FAMILY

GOD warned Noah and his family of an imminent coming flood and instructed him how to prepare to survive it. *By faith Noah, being warned of God of things not seen as yet, moved with fear, prepared an ark to the saving of his house; by the which he condemned the world, and became heir of the righteousness which is by faith.* (Hebrews 11:7) Every time we obey God's warning, we **save** our lives.

LOT & HIS FAMILY

GOD warned Lot and his family specifically of the coming destruction of SODOM and GOMORRAH and told them to flee. *And Lot went out, and spake unto his sons in law, which married his daughters, and said, up, get you out of this place; for the LORD will destroy this city. But he seemed as one that mocked unto his sons in law.* (Genesis 19:14). Every time we disobey GOD's warning, we always pay the price for the consequences.

PHARAOH OF EGYPT

GOD warned the Pharaoh of Egypt, through Joseph the dreamer, of the coming famine and used Joseph to prepare stores of grain during the seven years of plenty, which saved Egypt and Joseph's family when a seven-year famine followed the times of plenty. *And there shall arise after them seven years of famine; and all the plenty shall be forgotten in the land of Egypt; and the famine shall consume the land; And the plenty shall not be known in the land by reason of that famine following; for it shall be very grievous.* (Genesis 41:30-31). Until we obey God's warnings, we will be vulnerable to the impeding destruction.

THE ISRAELITES

GOD warned the Israelites living in Egypt as slaves that the "angel of death" would kill all the first-born of every family and that they must protect themselves and their families by placing the blood of a lamb over the door posts, so the angel would "pass over" them. *For the LORD will pass through to smite the Egyptians; and when he seeth the blood upon the lintel, and on the two side posts, the LORD will pass over the door, and will not suffer the destroyer to come in unto your houses to smite you.* (Exodus 12:23). Every time God gives any warning, it might take some time, but it will eventually happen.

THE PEOPLE OF NINEVAH

GOD warned the **sinful**, wicked people of Nineveh, the capital city of Assyria, of pending destruction through Jonah. When they repented, the judgment was averted and did not come for a number of years. *And Jonah began to enter into the city a day's journey, and he cried, and said, Yet forty days, and Nineveh shall be overthrown. So the people of Nineveh believed God, and proclaimed a fast, and put on sackcloth, from the greatest of them even to the least of them.* (Jonah 3:4-9) It is recorded that when the people of Nineveh fasted, their animals also fasted with them.

WHAT ARE WE SAYING?

It is inevitable to avert God's warning, especially if we disobey it. God's warning is for us to be informed of God's coming judgment. Repent of our sins and change the way we live our lives. We will be judged and held accounbtable for all our works here on Earth—good or evil.

NOW REPEAT THIS PRAYER ALOUD WITH ME:

Say Lord Jesus, I accept you today as my lord and as my savior. Forgive me of my sins, wash me with your blood. Right now I believe I am sanctified, I am saved and I am free. I am free from the power of sin to serve the Lord Jesus. Thank you, Lord, for saving me.

You are now a born again Christian.

SUMMARY OF CHAPTER 1

Son of man, I have made thee a watchman unto the house of Israel: therefore hear the word at my mouth, and give them warning from me.
Ezekial 3:17

God warns us through several channels, including: the prophet, spiritual literatures, visions, revelation and dreams.

THROUGH THE PROPHET: God uses all his prophets to issue divine judgment and warning to all. *Son of man, I have made thee a watchman unto the house of Israel: therefore hear the word at my mouth, and give them warning from me.* (Ezekial 3:17)

THROUGH DREAMS & VISIONS: *For God speaketh once, yea twice, yet man perceiveth it not. In a dream, in a vision of the night, when deep sleep falleth upon men, in slumberings upon the bed.* (Job 33:14-15) God uses our dreams and visions to warn us about a coming blessing and against impending danger. *After these things the word of the Lord came unto Abram in a vision, saying, Fear not, Abram: I am thy shield, and thy exceeding great reward.* (Genesis 15:1)

THROUGH REVELATION: Every time we are in the SPIRIT, we HEAR from GOD, for as long as we operate in the SPIRIT, we have the advantage to HEAR from GOD. *I was in the Spirit on the Lord's day, and heard behind me a great voice, as of a trumpet.* (Revelation 1:10)

"BEWARE"

Take inventory of what GOD has been saying to you through your DREAMS.

CHAPTER 2
THE PURPOSE OF REDEMPTION

Christ hath redeemed us from the curse of the law,
being made a curse for us; for it is written,
Cursed is everyone that hanged on a tree.
That the blessing of Abraham might come
on the gentiles through Jesus Christ,
that we might receive the promise
of the Spirit through faith.
Galations 3:13-14

WHAT DOES IT MEAN "TO BE REDEEMED"?

What is redemption?

The word redeem is defined as the act of delivering a sinner from bondage and punishment by means of a substitutionary sacrifice or through the payment of a ransom. This deliverance includes the excavation of sin. At times, the word redeem may also include the concept of purchasing or buying back something which was formerly possessed. The term redemption refers to the act of redeeming or to the state of being redeemed.

God's redemption purpose therefore refers to God's plan of salvation through His acts of redemption. Each one of God's past redemptive acts is part of the development of His plan to restore lost sinners into communion and relationship with Him. Immediately after man sinned and became subject to all misery and condemnation, God began to reveal to man His thoughts of peace and reconciliation.

The first promise made with Adam and Eve contained the essence and substance of the entire plan of salvation, even though it was only in its elementary form. God's gracious redemptive plan was increasingly revealed with the progression of time. The Old Testament promises, types and messianic prophecies all pointed forward to the coming of the Messiah, in whom God's purposes of redemption would be ultimately fulfilled. These means shadowed forth, to the Old Testament saints, the one and only way of salvation through the substitutionary death of the Lamb of God. With the eyes of faith, they rejoiced to see the promised Messiah, and in Him they obtained the blessings of **santification, justification and the forgiveness of sins**.

Redemptive history climaxes with the shedding of the blood of the Son of God on the cross. His precious blood was the necessary price for redeeming sinners from the state of condemnation and death. The Christological focus of redemptive history does not end with Christ's first coming, however, but it also includes the manifestations of His grace and mercy in this present age. And it anticipates His second advent, when He will make a final restoration of all things unto Himself.

THE PRICE OF REDEMPTION

There was an infinite debt that was owed to God by reason of sin, but there was no sinner who could pay the price to redeem himself or others. All were condemned and all were under wrath and there was none who had anything to offer God to pay for his sin. The redemption of the soul is so precious and costly that it required a payment that was of infinite value and worth (see Psalms 49:7-8).

Divine justice required a price that was far beyond human comprehension and expression. The necessary price of redemption was the precious blood of the Lamb of God! God gave His most treasured possession to purchase His people back to Himself. The cost was so great, and yet He spared not His Son, His only Son, and the Son of His love, that He might redeem sinners from the curse of the law. Every believer is bought with the price of the shed blood of Jesus Christ. Therefore, God can now speak tender words of love to their hearts, *"I have redeemed thee...thou art Mine."* (Isaiah 43:1) He loved sinners and bought sinners that they might be His eternal and prized possession.

WHAT ARE WE SAYING?

In a nutshell, "LOVE" is the reason behind REDEMPTION. For God so loved the world, that He sent His only begotten son to REDEEM man from perishing and to restore ETERNAL LIFE unto man.

For God so loved the world, that he gave his only begotten Son, that whosoever believeth in him should not perish, but have everlasting life. For God sent not his Son into the world to condemn the world, but that the world through him might be saved.
John 3:16-17

Although man fell short of the glory of God (Romans 3:23), redemption was God's ultimate plan for man. The **reason for redemption** is so that we all might enjoy genuine SALVATION and the joy of eternal life with Jesus Christ in HEAVEN.

HINDERANCES TO REDEMPTION & REPENTANCE

Sin is the only known barrier that will stop all of us from experiencing genuine SALVATION.

What is sin, one may ask?

Someone said S.I.N means Satan Identification Number. I do not disagree, but it is incomplete. In my definition, sin is disobeying God's words and commandments. Every time you operate outside the boundaries of the commandment of God, you are committing sin.

He that committeth sin is of the devil; for the devil sinneth from the beginning. For this purpose the son of God was manifested that he might destroy the works of the devil.
Job 3:25

He that covereth his sins shall not prosper: but whoso confesseth and forsaketh them shall have mercy.
Proverbs 28:13

Concerning **divine judgment,** as long as we cover up our sins, we will be exposed and judged—even while we are still alive. Just like the Bible say, *"he that covered his sin shall not prosper."*

Despite what David said in Psalms 51:3—*For I acknowledge my transgressions and my sin is ever before me*—we must not take the purpose of the life and death of Jesus in vain. Man by nature was born in sin, David attested. *Behold I was shapen in iniquity; and in sin did my mother conceive me.* (Psalms 51:5)

WHO IS A SINNER?

We were all born sinners. Therefore we are all sinners.

Examine yourselves, whether ye be in the faith; prove your own selves. Know ye not your own selves, how that Jesus Christ is in you, except ye be reprobates?
2 Corinthians 13:5

Although most faith people live in denial about the work of the flesh, from my own scriptural understanding, everyone operating within the scope of Galatians 5:20-21 is classified as a sinner.

*Now the works of the flesh are manifest,
which are these; Adultery, fornication, uncleanness,
lasciviousness, Idolatry, witchcraft, hatred, variance,
emulations, wrath, strife, seditions, heresies, Envyings,
murders, drunkenness, revellings, and such like: of the
which I tell you before, as I have also told you in time
past, that they which do such things shall not
inherit the kingdom of God.*
Galatians 5:20-21

Further supporting scripture...

*But the fearful, and unbelieving,
and the abominable, and murderers,
and whoremongers, and sorcerers, and idolaters,
and all liars, shall have their part in the lake
which burneth with fire and brimstone:
which is the second death.*
Revelation 21:8

WHO, THEREFORE, IS A SINNER?

In my opinion, all that have not acknowledged Jesus Christ as Lord and savior are sinners. The Bible says God heareth not sinners. Without contradiction all unbelievers are sinners. Unless God has mercy, most unbelievers will not make eternity in heaven.

Furthermore, all liars are sinners before the Almighty God. Lying is a very serious sin, simply because it leads to poverty and shame. Lying destroys our great future. Someone I know very well lied so much to himself, he made himself a beggar and frustrated the will of God over his life. The list of who is a sinner is a very complex and long list; it includes all who participate in the following: adultery, fornication, uncleanness, lasciviousness, idolatry, witchcraft, hatred, variance, emulations, wrath, strife, seditions, heresies, envyings, murders, drunkenness, revellings.

HOW DO I COME OUT OF SIN?

You must **REPENT** and **CONFESS** THE LORD JESUS CHRIST!

The word says, *"As many as received him, to them gave he power to become the sons of God, even to them that believe on his name."* (John 1:12)

STEPS TO OVERCOME THE LIFESTYLE OF SIN

—YOU MUST BE BORN AGAIN!

—**GENUINE REPENTANCE:** GOD will give you as many chances as you desire. The truth is, we must take advantage of those opportunities to truly come out of **sin**.

—To qualify for **salvation**, do the following sincerely:

1) Acknowledge that you are a sinner and that He died for you. (Romans 3:23)

2) Repent of your sins. (Acts 3:19, Luke 13:5, 2 Peter 3:9)

3) Believe in your heart that Jesus died for your sin. (Romans 10:10)

4) Confess Jesus as the Lord over your life. (Romans 10:10, Acts 2:21)

NOW REPEAT THIS PRAYER AFTER ME:

"Lord Jesus, I accept you today, as my Lord and my savior. Forgive me of my sins, wash me with your blood. Right now, I believe I am sanctified, I am saved, I am free. I am free from the power of sin to serve the Lord Jesus. Thank you, Lord, for saving me. Amen."

Congratulations.

YOU ARE NOW A BORN AGAIN CHRISTIAN!

REVIEW

In my view, Understanding Divine Judgment means: **understanding how God wants us to live here on Earth, based on the scriptures**. We must all identify the primary source of our prevailing challenges and the sins that easily beset us. We must find out what we have been doing wrong and what attracts GOD'S JUDGMENT.

> *Wherefore seeing we also are compassed*
> *about with so great a cloud of witnesses,*
> *let us lay aside every weight,*
> *and the sin which doth so easily beset us,*
> *and let us run with patience the race*
> *that is set before us.*
> **Hebrews 12:1**

GOD'S JUDGMENT IS COMING!

Unless we repent, confess and forsake our sins, there is an awaiting divine judgment that we cannot escape. All the frustration we have endured in life is because we have misplaced our trust.

Commit your ways into the hand of Jesus Christ. Trust also in Him and you shall be free.

Practice to pray and ask the mediator of the new convenant–Jesus Christ & the Holy Spirit—to make intercession for you. We must activate the presence of the Holy Spirit in our lives if we desire to live holy.

CONDITIONS TO RECEIVE THE HOLY SPIRIT

1) REPENTANCE: Repent, every one of you, in the name of Jesus Christ. For the remission of sins and ye shall receive the gift of the Holy Ghost.

2) BE BAPTIZED: Be baptized, every one of you, in the name of Jesus Christ. For the remission of sins and ye shall receive the gift of the Holy Ghost.

3) CONFESS OF YOUR SIN: If we confess our sins, He is faithful and just to forgive us our sins, and to cleanse us from all unrighteousness.

4) ACKNOWLEDGEMENT: Acknowledge that you are a sinner and that Jesus Christ died for your sins. (Romans 3:23)

5) BORN AGAIN: Jesus answered and said unto him, Verily, verily, I say unto thee, Except a man be born again, he cannot see the kingdom of God. Nicodemus saith unto him, How can a man be born when he is old? can he enter the second time into his mother's womb, and be born? Jesus answered, Verily, verily, I say unto thee, Except a man be born of water and of the Spirit, he cannot enter into the kingdom of God. That which is born of the flesh is flesh; and that which is born of the Spirit is spirit. Marvel not that I said unto thee, Ye must be born again. The wind bloweth where it listeth, and thou hearest the sound thereof, but canst not tell whence it cometh, and whither it goeth: so is every one that is born of the Spirit. (John 3:3-8)

PRAYER POINTS TO ACTIVATE THE PRESENCE OF THE HOLY SPIRIT

—Holy Spirit, reveal yourself to me, in the Name of Jesus.

—Holy Spirit, crush every daily habit of sin, in the Name of Jesus.

—Holy Spirit, become my companion today, in the Name of Jesus.

—Holy Spirit, grant me access, in the Name of Jesus.

—Power of God, grant me the GRACE to live right for Jesus Christ.

—Hand of God, deliver me from sin, in the Name of Jesus.

—Fire of God, burn every sinful thoughts from my mind, in the Name of Jesus.

—I proclaim authority over every prevailing sin in my life, in Jesus Name.

—I destroy every root of sin in my life, in Jesus Name.

—Sin shall not have dominion over my life, in the Name of Jesus.

—Lord God, emphasize genuine repentance over my spirit man, in the Name of Jesus

—Holy Spirit, revive and rekindle your fire of revival inside of me, in the Name of Jesus.

—Power of God, hijack the controlling forces oppressing my life, in the Name of Jesus.

—Blood of Jesus, take over my life, in the Name of Jesus.

—O Lord, baptize me with the gift of the Holy Spirit.

—Holy Spirit, breathe afresh upon my life, in the Name of Jesus.

—Holy Spirit, take possession of my will, in the Name of Jesus.

—Holy Spirit, make yourself real to me, in the name of Jesus.

—Holy Spirit, fan your revival fire upon my life, in the name of Jesus.

PRAYER POINTS TO OVERCOME TRIALS BY THE HELP OF THE HOLY SPIRIT

1) Father Lord, deliver me from this present trial, in the Name of Jesus.

2) Almighty Father, break me out of this present obscurity, in the Name of Jesus.

3) Holy Spirit, help me to overcome this trial, in Jesus Name.

4) Holy Spirit, speak to me, in the Name of Jesus.

5) Holy Spirit, minister to my subconscious spirit, in the Name of Jesus.

6) Fire of God, burn down every mountain of difficulty, in the Name of Jesus.

7) Holy Ghost, baptize me with your fire, in the Name of Jesus.

8) Holy Spirit, go before me and favor me in this present challenge, in the Name of Jesus.

9) Spirit of God, grant me liberty and freedom by the fire of the Holy Spirit, in the Name of Jesus.

10) Father Lord, intervene on my behalf, in the Name of Jesus.

11) Ancient of day, liberate me this season, in the Name of Jesus.

12) Immortal redeemer, bring me higher above these prevailing changes.

13) Lord God, turn this present obstacale into my miracle, in the Name of Jesus.

14) Fire of God, break down these obstacles for me, in the Name of Jesus.

15) Holy Spirit, favor me in, Jesus Name.

16) Holy Spirit. release me from this challenge, in the Name of Jesus.

17) Holy Spirit, become my compionion, in Jesus Name.

18) Holy Spirit, represent me in this matter.

19) Holy Spirit, elevant me beyond my own immagination, in the Name of Jesus.

20) Holy Spirit, do not allow my enemies to truimph over my life, in the Name of Jesus.

21) Fire of God, protect me, in the Name of Jesus.

22) Fire of God, destroy my enemies, in the Name of Jesus.

23) Fire of God, build a wall around me, in the Name of Jesus.

24) Fire of God, expose my enemies, in the Name of Jesus.

25) Fire of God, prove yourself, in the Name of Jesus.

26) Holy Spirit, represent me in jesus name.

27) Holy Spirit, release your boldnes into my life.

28) Holy Spirit, grant me signs and wonders.

29) Holy Spirit, make me a living wonder in my lifetime.

30) Holy Spirit, turn my life around, in the Name of Jesus.

31) Holy Spirit, I will not remain at this level, in the Name of Jesus.

32) Spirit of God, lift me higher, in the mighty Name of Jesus.

33) Angels of God, minister unto me, in the Name of Jesus.

34) Hand of God, separate me this season, in the Name of Jesus.

SUMMARY OF CHAPTER TWO

The Bible says, "for God so LOVED the world He GAVE..." (John 3:16)

We are **redeemed** and **delivered** from our sins by the precious blood of Jesus. Let this truth become our evidence against all satanic manipulation. Satan has been defeated on the cross a very long time ago, therefore he has no power to seduce, harass nor torture any of us. Everything "GOOD" that has ever happened in your life is the by the hand of GOD—and everything "BAD" was thanks to Satan and his cohorts.

YOU MUST BE BORN AGAIN—

Jesus answered and said unto him, Verily, verily, I say unto thee, Except a man be born again, he cannot see the kingdom of God. Nicodemus saith unto him, How can a man be born when he is old? can he enter the second time into his mother's womb, and be born? Jesus answered, Verily, verily, I say unto thee, Except a man be born of water and of the Spirit, he cannot enter into the kingdom of God. That which is born of the flesh is flesh; and that which is born of the Spirit is spirit. Marvel not that I said unto thee, Ye must be born again. The wind bloweth where it listeth, and thou hearest the sound thereof, but canst not tell whence it cometh, and whither it goeth: so is every one that is born of the Spirit.
John 3:3-8

You've been redeemed by the blood of Jesus. Therefore, spiritualize and sanctify your life to refect the same.

CHAPTER 3
SALVATION—THE ESCAPE ROUTE INTO ETERNAL LIFE

How shall we escape, if we neglect so great salvation; which at the first began to be spoken by the Lord, and was confirmed unto us by them that heard him.
Hebrews 2:3

WHAT IS SALVATION?

Salvation means deliverance from our sins and sickness and redemption of our soul. There is no other way we all can be saved except by the name of Jesus Christ of Nazareth.

Neither is there salvation in any other: for there is none other name under heaven given among men, whereby we must be saved.
ACTS 4:12

What must I do to be SAVED?

YOU MUST BE BORN AGAIN!

The word says, *"as many as received him, to them gave He power to become the sons of God, even to them that believe on his name."* (John 1:12)

There is no righteous and perfect man on Earth. all of us have our short comings.

*For all have sinned,
and come short of the glory of God.*
Romans 3:23

EXAMPLES FROM THE HOLY BIBLE

1) Jacob committed adultery and cheated on his wives.

2) Peter had a temper problem at one point, coupled with his lack of faith in God.

3) Moses and Paul were murderers.

4) Thomas doubted Jesus Christ.

5) Jonah disobeyed God and ran away.

6) Miriam gossiped with Aaron concerning Moses' Ethopian wife.

7) While Martha worried, Rachel envied her sister and was anxious about bearing a child.

None of us is qualified before the righteous God. There is only one way to salvation.

WHEN ARE WE SAVED?

We are saved when we confess the Lord Jesus with our mouth, and believe with our heart. (Romans 10:10)

And it shall come to pass that whosoever shall call on the name of the Lord, shall be saved.
Acts 2:21

Neither is there salvation in any other; for there is none other name under heaven given among men, whereby we must be saved.
Acts 4:12

ARE YOU SAVED?

You must be SAVED not from the mouth but from the HEART genuinely—this is SALVATION.

We are saved when we confess the Lord Jesus and believe with our heart. *For with the heart man believed unto righteousness, and with the mouth confession is made unto salvation.* (Romans 10:10)

For the wages of sin is death; but the gift of God is eternal life through Jesus Christ our Lord.
Romans 6:23

If you take inventory of your life and the life of a few people around you, you will agree with me

that it is time to give up sin. It is time to change the way you live.

For sin shall not have dominion over you:
for ye are not under the law, but under grace.
Romans 6:14

Sin is a weapon of the devil to afflict your life with misery, stagnation and difficulties. All I have said from the beginning will remain a mystery until you commit it into practice.

If you have not given your life to Jesus Christ, do so now. Give your life to Christ. Know the truth today for yourself! The truth is that Jesus died for your sins. And because He died, you must be ALIVE and make eternity (SAFE and SAVED).

WHAT MUST I DO TO BE SAVED?

To be SAVED you must be BORN AGAIN.

The word says, *"as many as received him, to them gave He power to become the sons of God, even to them that believe on his name."* (John 1:12)

1) Acknowledge that you are a sinner and that He died for you. (Romans 3:23)

2) Repent of your sins. (Acts 3:19, Luke 13:5,

2 Peter 3:9)

3) Believe in your heart that Jesus died for your sins. (Romans 10:10)

4) Confess Jesus as the Lord over your life. (Romans 10:10, Acts 2:21)

Now repeat this prayer after me:

Say Lord Jesus, I accept you today, as my Lord and my savior. Forgive me of my sins, wash me with your blood. Right now, I believe I am sanctified, I am saved, I am free. I am free from the power of sin, to serve the Lord Jesus. Thank you Lord for saving me. Amen.

Congratulations. You are now...

A BORN AGAIN CHRISTIAN.

Again I say to you—CONGRATULATIONS!

I adjure you to watch the Spirit of God bear witness with your Spirit, confirming His word with signs following. The word says The Spirit itself beareth witness with our spirit, that we are the children of God.

PRAYER POINTS TO REVERSE ALL SPIRITUAL JUDGMENT AGAINST YOU

1) Father Lord, deliver me from divine judgment, in the Name of Jesus.

2) Almighty Father, break me through all impending dangers, in the Name of Jesus.

3) Holy Spirit, help me to be saved, in Jesus Name.

4) Holy Spirit, speak to me, in the Name of Jesus.

5) Holy Spirit, minister to my subconscious spirit, in the Name of Jesus.

6) Fire of God, burn down every mountain of difficulty, in the Name of Jesus.

7) Holy Ghost, baptize me with your fire, in the Name of Jesus.

8) God of heaven, go before me and favor me in this present challenge, in the Name of Jesus.

9) Spirit of God, grant me liberty and freedom by the fire of the Holy Spirit, in the Name of Jesus.

10) Father Lord, intervene on my behalf, in the Name of Jesus.

11) Ancient of day, liberate me this season, in the Name of Jesus.

12) Immortal redeemer, bring me higher above these prevailing changes.

13) Lord God, turn this present obstacale into my miracle, in the Name of Jesus.

14) Fire of God, break down these obstacles for me, in the Name of Jesus.

15) Holy Spirit, favor me, in Jesus Name.

16) Holy Spirit. release me from this challenge, in the Name of Jesus.

17) Holy Spirit, become my compionion, in Jesus Name.

18) Holy Spirit, represent me in all my present challenges.

19) Holy Spirit, elevate me beyond my own immaginetion, in the Name of Jesus.

20) Holy Spirit, do not allow my enemies to truimph over my life, in the Name of Jesus.

21) Fire of God, protect me, in the Name of Jesus.

22) Fire of God, destroy my enemies, in the Name of Jesus.

23) Fire of God, build a wall around me, in the Name of Jesus.

24) Fire of God, expose my enemies, in the Name of Jesus.

25) Fire of God, prove yourself, in the Name of Jesus.

26) Holy Spirit, represent me in jesus name.

27) Holy Spirit, release your boldness into my life.

28) Holy Spirit, grant me signs and wonders.

29) Holy Spirit, make me a living wonder in my lifetime.

30) Holy Spirit, turn my life around, in the Name of Jesus.

31) Holy Spirit, I will not remain at this level, in the Name of Jesus.

32) Spirit of God, lift me higher, in the mighty Name of Jesus.

33) Angels of God, minister unto me, in the Name of Jesus.

34) Hand of God, separate me this season, in the Name of Jesus.

345 Father Lord, fight all my invincible battles, in the Name of Jesus.

CONCLUSION

Shall not the judge of all the Earth do right?
Genesis 18:25

God's divine judgment is based on our present action and deed in life. We are absolutely responsible for the outcome of all our actions, work and deeds (evil, good or bad).

God's divine judgment is based on the spiritual principles of action and judgment (cause and effect), where the intentions of our heart and the actions of our hand are judged by God. Beware, God is spirit—and we must worship Him in spirit and in truth.

The Bible says, *"evil must bow before the good."* Desire to be known for your good qualities. Every time you do good, it registers in heaven.

The divine judgment of God is inevitable. It may be delayed, but it will surely catch up with you. Therefore, desire to give your life to Jesus Christ and become a new creature.

TIME TO PLAN YOUR LIFE?

*And as it is appointed unto men once to die,
but after this the judgment.*
Hebrews 9:27

We must all make accurate and precise plans for our life. A wise man once said, **"If you live casually, you will become a casualty."**

In my own scriptural understanding, it takes a good heart to live right. You may say I got hold of this book by coincidence or by mistake! Hold on to the truth of what we have been saying all along. You must plan your life. The reason for all the worries and frustration is because there is no genuine plan to confront those prevailing challenges.

If you are not a Born Again Christian, we can help you receive genuine salvation.

*Therefore if any man be in Christ,
he is a new creature: old things are passed away;
behold, all things are become new.*
2 Corinthians 5:17

*Say Lord Jesus, I accept you today, as my Lord and
my savior. Forgive me of my sins, wash me with your blood.
Right now, I believe I am sanctified, I am saved, I am free.
I am free from the power of sin, to serve the Lord Jesus.
Thank you Lord for saving me. Amen.*

Chapter 3   Salvation—The Escape Route to Eternal Life

Congratulations. You are now...

    A BORN AGAIN CHRISTIAN.

Again I say to you—CONGRATULATIONS!

WHAT MUST I DO TO DETERMINE MY DIVINE VISITATION?

To determine divine visitation you must be BORN AGAIN! The word says, *"as many as received him, to them gave He power to become the sons of God, even to them that believe on his name."* (John 1:12)

To qualify for divine visitation, do the following sincerely:

1) Acknowledge that you are a sinner and that He died for you. (Romans 3:23)

2) Repent of your sins. (Acts 3:19, Luke 13:5, 2 Peter 3:9)

3) Believe in your heart that Jesus died for your sins. (Romans 10:10)

4) Confess Jesus as the Lord over your life. (Romans 10:10, Acts 2:21)

Now repeat this prayer after me:

Say Lord Jesus, I accept you today as my Lord and my savior. Forgive me of my sins, wash me with your blood. Right now, I believe I am sanctified, I am saved, I am free. I am free from the power of sin, to serve the Lord Jesus. Thank you, Lord, for saving me. Amen.

Congratulations. You are now a BORN AGAIN CHRISTIAN!

Again I say to you—CONGRATULATIONS!

I adjure you to watch the Spirit of God bear witness with your Spirit, confirming His word with signs following. The word says, *"the Spirit itself beareth witness with our spirit, that we are the children of God."* (Romans 8:16) Join a Bible-believing church or join us on our Wednesdays healing and Sunday miracle worship services at 343 Sanford Avenue, Newark, NJ 07106.

DECISION KEYS

1) Nothing changes until you make up your mind.

2) Decision is the gateway to deliverance.

3) Until you decide, no one will decide for you.

4) Your prosperity is proportional to your decisions.

5) The decision you make will determine the future you will create

6) Decision creates future and fulfills destinies.

7) Decision beautifies our future.

8) Decision keeps you out of trouble.

9) Decision exempts you from evil.

10) Decision gurantees eternity.

11) You can only go far in life by your faith decisions.

12) You are poor because you made such decisions

13) Make a decision and change your life.

14) Life changing decisions are a function of quality information.

15) Success in life is a function of decision.

16) Life experiences are full of decisions.

17) Decisions change destinies.

18) Never settle for information—always look for revelation.

19) You are where you are today based on your last decision.

20) Information is crucial in decision making.

21) Decision makers rule the world.

22) You can rule your world with quality decisions.

23) As long as you decide rightly, Satan cannot harrass you.

Chapter 3   Salvation—The Escape Route to Eternal Life

WISDOM KEYS

—If you train your mind to reason, it will train your hands to earn money.

—It is absurd to use the money of the heathen to build the kingdom of the living God.

—Every Ministry reveals its agenda and VISION either at the beginning or at the end.

—Be careful of your life. It is your First Ministry.

—Everyone is waiting for you to change your mind. Until you change your thinking, nothing changes around you.

—Multiple academic degrees in other disciplines gave me the chance to think and reason.

—Whatever anyone is thinking at any time reveals what is inside of their heart.

—All planned events are the product of meditation.

—Every event is designed for a designated timeline.

—Wisdom is your ability to think, to create and invent.

— If you can think wisely enough, you will come out

of debt.

—The distance between you and your success is your innovative and creative ability to think well.

—Success is the result of hard work, commitment, resolve and determined learning from past mistakes and failings.

—If you organize your mind, you have organized your life and destiny.

—There is a thin line between success and failure.

—Wealth is your ability to think, power is your ability to reason and success is your ability to be informed.

—If you can make use of your mind by thinking and reasoning, God will make use of your life and destiny.

—Reflect, reason, think and be Great.

—Famous people are born of woman.

—That you will make it is your intention, that you will survive is your resolve, that you will succeed with changes is your determination, personal efforts and hard work.

—No man was born a failure.

—Lack of vision is the result of failure.

—Working with mental patients encourages and aspire me to be a productive observant and dedicated to my assignment.

—Successful people are not magicians. It is the will-power, combined with hard work and determination and a resolve to succeed, that make them succeed.

—In the unequivocal state of the mind, intention is not a location or a position. It is the state of the mind.

—So many people think that they think.

—The mind is used to think, to reflect and to reason.

—You will remain blind with your eyes open until you can see with your mind by thinking.

—There is no favoritism in accurate and precise calculation.

—Although knowledge is power, information is the key and gateway to a great future.

—It will take the hand of God to move the hand of man.

—With the backing of the great wise God, nothing will

disconnect you from your inheritance.

—As long as you have wisdom and understanding of God, Satan and evil cannot manipulate your life and destiny.

—You have come this far in life by your own judgment and the decisions you made in the past. Now lean in and listen to God for another dimension of greatness.

—Great people are ordinary people. It is extra ordinary efforts and the price of sacrifice that produces greatness in them.

—As a mental direct care worker, I saw a great pastor and a motivational speaker within myself.

—A menial job does not reduce your self-worth. Until you resolve to achieve greatness and see greatness in all you do, you will never count in your community.

—The principle of Jesus will solve your gambling and addiction problems.

—The man of Jesus will lead you into heaven.

—Everyone has their self-appraisal and what they think about you. Until you discover yourself, other opinions about you will alter the real you.

—Supervisors and directors are just positions in the chain of command in a work place.

—Never allow your supervisor on a job to alter your opinion about yourself.

—Everyone can come out of debt if they make up their mind.

—The fact that I am not a decision-maker at my work place does not diminish my contribution to my world.

—Self-encouragement and determination is a resolve of the heart.

—If you are determined to make a difference and do the things that make a difference, you will eventually make a difference.

—Good things do not come easy.

—Short cuts will cut your life short.

—Those who look ahead move ahead.

—Life is all about making an impact. In your lifetime strive to make an impact in your community.

—Make friends and connect with people who are moving ahead of you in life.

—If you can look around well, you have come a long way in your life, made a lot of difference and realized a lot of success in life.

—If you are my old friend, hurry up to reach out to me before I become a stranger to you.

—I am blessed with inspirations from God that changed my interpretation of the world around me.

—I thought I was stagnant and lonely until I looked around and noticed my children running around and my wife cooking in the kitchen.

—You will be a better person if you understand the characteristics of your personality like your mood swings, attitudes and habits.

—It is the seed of love you sow into the heart of a child and a woman that you reap in due time.

—Love is not selfish.

—Love shares everything, including the concealed secrets of the mind.

—As long as you have a prayer life and a Bible, you will never feel lonely in the race of life.

—When good friends disconnect from you, let them

go. They might have seen something new in a different direction.

—Confidence in yourself and in God is the only way to bring you out of captivity

—Never train a child to waste his or her time.

—The mind is the greatest asset of a great future.

—You walk by common sense, run by principles and fly by instruction.

—Those who become successful in life did it by self-determination, hard work and learning from past failures.

—Most successful people are lonely people. No one renders help to them, believing they are already successful. Except when they seek for more knowledge and information, they are all alone.

—I exercise my judgment and make a decision every minute of the day. Decisions are crucial, critical and vital with reference to your future.

—So many people wish for a great future. You can only work towards a great future.

—Your celebrity status began when you discovered your talent. What are you good at? Work at it with all your commitment.

—Prayers will sustain you, but the wisdom of God will prosper you.

—When I met Oyedepo, his teachings changed my perspective. But when I met Ibiyeomie, his teaching changed my perception.

CHAPTER 4
PRAYER OF SALVATION

Have you accepted Jesus Christ as your personal lord and savior?

Salvation is deliverance from sins and redemption of your soul. As long as you genuinely repent of all your sins, God will restore your life beyond your own imagination.

WHAT IS SALVATION?

Salvation means deliverance from your sins and sickness and redemption of your soul. There is no other way we all can be saved except by the Name of Jesus Christ of Nazareth.

> *Neither is there salvation in any other:*
> *for there is none other name under heaven*
> *given among men, whereby we must be saved.*
> **Acts 4:12**

I am glad you have read this book all the way from the beginning to this point. All I have said from the beginning will remain a mystery until you commit it into practice.

What must I do to receive SALVATION?

TO RECEIVE SALVATION YOU MUST BE BORN AGAIN

The word says as many as received Him, to them gave He power to become the sons of God. Even to them that believe on His name.

To qualify for SALVATION, do the following sincerely:

1) Acknowledge that you are a sinner and that He died for you. (Romans 3:23)

2) Repent of your sins. (Acts 3:19, Luke 13:5, 2 Peter 3:9)

3) Believe in your heart that Jesus died for your sin. (Romans 10:10)

4) Confess Jesus as the Lord over your life. (Romans 10:10, Acts 2:21)

NOW REPEAT THIS PRAYER AFTER ME:
Say Lord Jesus, I accept you today, as my Lord and my savior. Forgive me of my sins, wash me with your blood. Right now, I believe I am sanctified, I am saved, I am free. I am free from the power of sin to serve the Lord Jesus. Thank you, Lord, for saving me. Amen.

Congratulations.

YOU ARE NOW A BORN AGAIN CHRISTAIN!

Again, I say to you—congratulations! I adjure you to watch the Spirit of God bear witness with your Spirit confirming His word with signs following. The word says the Spirit itself beareth witness with our spirit, that we are the children of God.

We are spirit, we live in a body and we have a soul. Salvation is not a one-time event. The Bible says, *"and be not conformed to this world, but be ye transformed by the renewing of your mind, that ye may prove what is that good and acceptable, and perfect, will of God."* (Romans 12:2)

We must join a bible-believing church and become active members of the local church. We must become soul winners and promote the great message of salvation and the great commission. We must help the less privileged and support the work of the kingdom of God.

MIRACLE CARE OUTREACH

"...But that the members should have the same care one for another"
1 Corinthians 12:25

We are all members of the body of Christ. Jesus commanded us to love our neighbor as ourselves. This includes caring for one another as a member of one body. True love is expressed in caring and giving. The word says, for God so Love He gave....

Reach out to someone in need of Jesus. Help someone in crisis find Christ. Look out and prove your love to Jesus by caring and inviting your friends and associates to find Jesus the Healer.

Invite your friends to our Home Care Cell Fellowship (Miracle Chapel Intl. Satellite Fellowship). We're in the U.S. at 33 Schley Street, Newark, New Jersey 07112. If you are in Nigeria—MIRACLE OF GOD MINISTRIES, aka "MIRACLE CHAPEL INTL." Mpama–Egbu-Owerri Imo state Nigeria.

Home Care Cell Fellowship Group meets every Tuesday at 6:00pm-7:00pm.

LIFE IS NOT ALL ABOUT DURATION, BUT IT'S ALL ABOUT DONATION

What does this statement mean?

Life consists not in accumulation of material wealth. (Luke 12:15) But it's all about liberality…i.e., what you can give and share with others. (Proverbs 11:25) When you live for others, you live forever—because you outlive your generation by the legacy you leave behind after you depart into glory to be with the Lord. But when you live for yourself, when you are reduced to SELF—you are easily forgotten when you die and depart in glory.

Permit me to admonish you today to live your life to be a blessing to a soul connected to you today. I want you to know that so many souls are connected and looking up to you, and through you so many souls will be saved and rescued from destruction. Will you disciple someone today to find Jesus Christ?

As a genuine Christian, it is your duty to evangelize Jesus Christ to all you meet on your way. Jesus is still in the healing business—Jesus is still doing miracles, from time of old to now. Therefore, tell someone about Jesus Christ today, disciple and bring them to Church. *Philip findeth Nathanael…* (John 1:45)

Please prove the sincerity of your love for God today, please become a soul winner. The dignity of your Christianity is hidden in your boldness to proclaim and evangelize Jesus Christ to all you meet on your way. There is a question mark on the integrity of your Christianity until you become a life soul winner. Invite someone to join us worship the Lord Jesus this coming Sunday.

MIRACLE OF GOD MINISTRIES
PILLARS OF THE COMMISSION

We Believe, Preach and Practice the following:

1) We believe and preach Salvation to every living human being.

2) We believe and preach Repentance and Forgiveness of sins.

3) We believe and preach the baptism of the Holy Spirit and Spiritual gifts.

4) We believe and teach Prosperity.

5) We believe and preach Divine Healing and Miracles—Signs and Wonder.

6) We believe and preach Faith.

7) We believe and proclaim the Power of God (Supernatural).

8) We believe and proclaim Praise and Worship to God.9) We believe and preach Wisdom.

10) We believe and preach Holiness (Consecration).

11) We believe and preach Vision.

12) We believe and teach the Word of God.

13) We believe and teach Success.

14) We believe and practice Prayer.

15) We believe and teach Deliverance.

These 15 stones form the Pillars of Our Commission. Become part of this church family and follow this great movement of God.

MY HEART FELT PRAYER FOR YOU

It is my burning desire for God to touch you through one of our teaching books, cd's. It also my personal desire for you encounter God for yourself.

Now let me Pray for you:
O Lord God! I beseech thee, and through
personal prayer intercession today that the Holy Spirit
will touch this precious soul reading this book and turn their
life around. Spirit of God possess this loved one.
Lord overcome all dominating controlling forces that
has prevailed over their lives. I come against all oppressive
though in Jesus Name. Henceforth; I pronounce you free,
from manipulation, intimidation and domination
of the wicked enemy called the devil. You are free from
all satanic harassment and assaults. Amen

FROM THE Judgment THRONE OF JEHOVAH

You must begin today to prepare for eternity. God's divine judgment is coming with divine speed.

Eternity is real, heaven is sure. Become interested in the heavenly race and book your name in the lamb book of life.

Therefore, turn unto God in supplication, in thanksgiving and in prayer, And God will turn in your favor.

ABOUT THE AUTHOR

Rev. Franklin N. Abazie is the founding and Presiding Pastor of Miracle of God Ministries, with headquarters in Newark, New Jersey USA and a branch church in Owerri-Imo State Nigeria. He is following the footsteps of one of his mentors, the healing evangelist Oral Roberts of the blessed memory. The Lord passed Oral Roberts' healing mantle two days before he went to be with the Lord at age 91 into the hands of healing evangelist Rev. Franklin N. Abazie in a vision.

In all his services, the Power and Presence of God is present to heal all in his audience. Rev. Abazie is an ordained man of God, with a Healing Ministry reviving the healing and miracle ministry of Jesus Christ of Nazareth.

Pastor Franklin N. Abazie, has been called by God with a unique mandate: **"THE MOMENT IS DUE TO IMPACT YOUR WORLD THROUGH THE REVIVAL OF THE HEALING AND MIRACLE MINISTRY OF JESUS CHRIST OF NAZARETH.**

"I AM SENDING YOU TO RESTORE HEALTH UNTO THEE AND I WILL HEAL THEE OF THY WOUNDS, SAID THE LORD OF HOST."

Rev. Abazie is a gifted, ardent teacher of the word of God, who operates also in the office of a Prophet, generating and attracting undeniable signs and wonders, special miracles and healings, with apostolic fireworks of the Holy Ghost. He is the founding and presiding senior Pastor of this fast growing Healing Ministry. He has written over 86 inspirational, healing and transforming books covering almost all aspects of divine healing and life. He is happily married and blessed with children.

BOOKS BY REV. FRANKLIN N. ABAZIE:

1) The Outcome of Faith
2) Understanding the Secret of Prevailing Prayers
3) Commanding Abundance
4) Understanding the Secret of the Man God Uses
5) Activating My Due Season
6) Overcoming Divine Verdicts
7) The Outcome of Divine Wisdom
8) Understanding God's Restoration Mandate
9) Walking In the Victory and Authority of the Truth
10) God's Covenant Exemption
11) Destiny Restoration Pillars
12) Provoking Acceptable Praise
13) Understanding Divine Judgment
14) Activating Angelic Re-enforcement
15) Provoking Un-Merited Favo
16) The Benefits of the Speaking Faith
17) Understanding Divine Arrangement
18) How to Keep Your Healing
19) Understanding the Mysteries of the Speaking Faith
20) Understanding the Mysteries of Prophetic Healing
21) Operating Under the Rules of Creative Healing
22) Understanding the Joy of Breakthrough
23) Understanding the Mystery of Breakthrough
24) Understanding Divine Prosperity
25) Understanding Divine Healing
26) Retaining Your Inheritance
27) Overcoming Confusing Spirit
28) Commanding Angelic Escorts

29) Enforcing Your Inheritance In Christ Jesus
30) Understanding Your Guardian Angels
31) Overcoming the Dominion of Sin
32) Understanding the Voice of God
33) The Outstanding Benefits of the Anointing
34) The Audacity of the Blood of Jesus
35) Walking in the Reality of the Anointing
36) Escaping the Nightmare of Poverty
37) Understanding Your Harvest Season
38) Activating Your Success Buttons
39) Overcoming the Forces of Darkness
40) Overcoming the Devices of the Devil
41) Overcoming Demonic Agents
42) Overcoming the Sorrows of Failure
43) Rejecting the Sorrows of Failure
44) Resisting the Sorrows of Poverty
45) Restoring Broken Marriages
46) Redeeming Your Days
47) The Force of Vision
48) Overcoming the Forces of Ignorance
49) Understanding the Sacrifice of Small Beginning
50) The Might of Small Beginning
51) Understanding the Mysteries of Prophesy
52) Overcoming Dream Nightmares
53) Breaking the Shackles of the Curse of the Law
54) Understanding the Joy of Harvest
55) Wisdom for Signs & Wonders
56) Wisdom for Generational Impact
57) Wisdom for Marriage Stability
58) Understanding the Number of Your Days

59) Enforcing Your Kingdom Rights
60) Escaping the Traps of Immoralities
61) Escaping the Trap of Poverty
62) Accessing Biblical Prosperity
63) Accessing True Riches in Christ
64) Silencing the Voice of the Accuser
65) Overcoming the Forces of Oppositions
66) Quenching the Voice of the Avenger
67) Silencing Demonic Prediction & Projection
68) Silencing Your Mocker
69) Understanding the Power of the Holy Ghost
70) Understanding the Baptism of Power
71) The Mystery of the Blood of Jesus
72) Understanding the Mystery of Sanctification
73) Understanding the Power of Holiness
74) Understanding the Forces of Purity & Righteousness
75) Activating the Forces of Vengeance
76) Appreciating the Mystery of Restoration
77) Overcoming the Projection & Prediction of the Enemy
78) Engaging the Mystery of the Blood
79) Commanding the Power of the Speaking Faith
80) Uprooting the Forces Against Your Rising
81) Overcoming Mere Success Syndrome
82) Understanding Divine Sentence
83) Understanding the Mystery of Praise
84) Understanding the Author of Faith
85) The Mystery of the Finisher of Faith
86) Attracting Supernatural Favor

MIRACLE OF GOD MINISTRIES
NIGERIA CRUSADE 2012

MIRACLE OF GOD MINISTRIES

NIGERIA CRUSADE

2012

MIRACLE OF GOD MINISTRIES

NIGERIA CRUSADE

2012

MIRACLE OF GOD MINISTRIES

NIGERIA CRUSADE 2012

www.ingramcontent.com/pod-product-compliance
Lightning Source LLC
Chambersburg PA
CBHW021450080526
44588CB00009B/775